COMING ALIVE

SINK THE
ARMADA!

STEWART ROSS

COMING ALIVE

SINK THE ARMADA!

SIR FRANCIS DRAKE
AND THE SPANISH ARMADA OF 1588

STEWART ROSS

Illustrated by
SUE SHIELDS

EVANS BROTHERS LIMITED

TO THE READER

Sink the Armada! is a story from history. There really was an Armada, and all the important events in this book really happened. The main people, like the Duke and Sir Francis Drake, were real, too. I added Tom, Carlos and Jack so the story is more interesting for children. To make it easy to read, all the speech is made up. I hope you enjoy *Sink the Armada!* and it makes you want to find out more about England at the time of Queen Elizabeth and the Spanish Armada.

Stewart Ross

For the pupils of Castle View School, Canvey Island

Published by Evans Brothers Limited
2A Portman Mansions, Chiltern Street
London W1M 1LE

British Library Cataloguing in Publication Data
Ross, Stewart
Sink the Armada! – (Coming alive)
1. Armada, 1588 – Juvenile literature
2. Great Britain – History – Elizabeth, 1558-1603 – Juvenile literature
I. Title
942'.055

First published 1999

Printed in Spain by Gráficas Reunidas, S.A.

ISBN 0 237 51959 3

CONTENTS

THE STORY SO FAR...

ENGLAND
When Elizabeth I became Queen of England (1558), she faced all sorts of problems. For example, because she was Protestant and wanted England to be Protestant, many Roman Catholics believed she had no right to take the throne. They thought Elizabeth's Roman Catholic cousin, Mary Queen of Scots, should rule England. Mary wanted this, too. In 1568 Mary was driven out of Scotland and became Elizabeth's prisoner. This put Elizabeth in a really tricky position, because Mary went on plotting to take over from her. Finally, in 1587, Elizabeth was so fed up with Mary she had her executed. Europe's Roman Catholics were horrified.

... AND SPAIN
No one was more horrified than King Philip II of Spain, Europe's most powerful Roman Catholic ruler. He had other reasons to dislike Elizabeth. For years English sailors, including the famous Sir Francis Drake, had attacked Spanish ships and bases in the New World.

Equally annoying, Elizabeth sent soldiers to help the Dutch, who were at war with Spain. By

1585 the fighting between Protestant England and Roman Catholic Spain had become a full-scale war, although war was not officially declared.

INVASION

England was not rich or powerful enough to invade Spain. But Spain's army and navy were certainly large enough to conquer England. The trouble was, Spain's army, led by the Duke of Parma, was in the Netherlands, while most of her ships were in Spanish waters. So King Philip planned to sail a large fleet from Spain to the Netherlands, pick up the Duke of Parma's army, and ferry it across the Channel to attack England. In 1587, the king's plan was set back when Drake raided the Spanish port of Cadiz and destroyed many ships and supplies. This made Philip all the more determined that his great fleet or 'armada' should sail the following summer. But first he had to find someone to command it...

PORTRAIT GALLERY

Sir Francis
Drake

Alonso, Duke of
Medina-Sidonia

Diego Flores

Carlos

Tom Barnecut

Duchess of
Medina-Sidonia

Old Jack
Pugh

Lord Charles
Howard

CHAPTER ONE

CAPTAIN-GENERAL OF THE OCEAN SEA

'You know,' said the Duke, looking out of the window at the rolling hills of his estate at San Lucar, 'I think I should have been a farmer. I like land. I like the look of the olive groves, the smell of the soil.'

**Alonso,
Duke of Medina-Sidonia**

The Duchess laughed. 'Just as well you like land,' she replied, 'since you own so much of it.' It was true. The thirty-seven-year-old Duke of Medina-Sidonia was one of the richest men in Europe. He didn't need to work, but when King

Philip appointed him Captain-General of the coast of Andalusia, in south-west Spain, he had been delighted. He felt he was doing his bit for king and country. Besides, he liked organising and was quite good at it, as he had showed defending Cadiz against the English the previous year. He turned towards his wife with a smile. 'You know what I mean, my dear.

Duchess of Medina-Sidonia

'I mean I prefer land to water. I enjoyed taking on that devil Drake and his infidel pirates because I hated the thought of them setting foot on Spain's holy soil.'

The Duchess moved to his side. 'Soon you won't have to worry about Drake or anyone else, Alonso. When Parma captures London, they'll all be dead or in prison.'

'As long as Parma's army gets to London,' said the Duke with a sigh. 'We've got to get the fleet to the Netherlands first.'

'And you don't have to worry about that, either,' said the Duchess, straightening the lace on

12

his collar. 'That's the sailors' job. You'll be safe here in Spain.'

'Thank goodness!' muttered the Duke. Remembering he had letters to write, he went off to find his secretary.

Carlos, the Duke of Medina-Sidonia's bald secretary, was an efficient, fussy man who had served the Duke's family for almost forty years. He made it his job not only to handle the Duke's correspondence, but to know everything that went on in his household. He knew, for example, that the fourth stable boy was courting the under-cook's daughter, and that the gold buttons on the Duke's new coat were worth just under a ducat each. So when a messenger arrived with a letter from the King, Carlos made sure it was he who put it in the Duke's hands.

Alonso, Duke of   Carlos
Medina-Sidonia

The secretary stood watching Duke Alonso's face as he broke the wax seal and began to read. After a few seconds, his forehead wrinkled into a frown. 'Not bad news, Your Grace?' Carlos asked sympathetically.

'Awful,' the Duke replied. 'The worst I have ever received.'

Carlos picked nervously at his fingernails. 'May I be so bold as to ask Your Grace what this news is?'

'You may,' said the Duke with a sigh. 'His Majesty wishes me to take command of the English invasion fleet. The Armada.' Carlos' jaw dropped in astonishment. 'I can't do it, Mister Secretary,' the Duke went on, checking the letter in case he had made a mistake. 'I'm not the right man. I can get the Armada ready for sea, but I cannot possibly sail with it. I am no naval commander. Besides, I get sea sick just looking at a ship.'

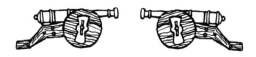

Carlos disliked the sea even more than his master. He was terrified that if the Duke went to sea, he might have to go too. So that afternoon he helped his master write a polite letter to the King explaining why the Duke of Medina-Sidonia was not a suitable commander for the Armada. He lacked experience of war and the sea; he was in debt, his health was poor, and he had no idea what the plans for the Armada were.

The King did not change his mind. In a second letter he told the Duke that, whether he liked it or

'His Majesty wishes me to take
command of the English invasion fleet.
The Armada.'

not, he was now Captain-General of the Ocean Sea and commander of the Armada.

'In which case, Mr Secretary,' the Duke said slowly, 'I suppose we'd better pack our things and get to the ships at Lisbon as quickly as possible.'

'I beg your pardon,' stammered Carlos, turning pale green and picking his fingernails more vigorously than ever, 'but did Your Grace say "we"?'

The Duke nodded. 'Of course, Mr Secretary! I could never manage without you. If I'm going to sea, then you're coming with me!'

CHAPTER TWO

'SMASH THEM AT SEA!'

The rumours started as soon as the first buds appeared on the wind-swept trees. A Dutch captain told drinkers in the Queen's Head tavern, Plymouth, that Spain was ready to attack England with two hundred ships. By the time the story reached London, the number of ships had risen to a thousand. A merchant returned from France to say that the King of Spain himself was coming in a golden galleon. And in mid-June a Cornish farmer reported seeing Spanish soldiers in the lane outside his cottage.

Sir Francis Drake

These, and many other hare-brained stories, all proved to be false alarms. 'Whistles in the wind,' Sir Francis Drake had called them. But it was now early July, and England's most famous sailor had just received reliable reports that the Armada finally had set sail.

Walking along the grassy slopes of Plymouth Hoe, Drake and his commander-in-chief, Lord

17

Charles Howard, were discussing the best way of beating off the Spanish attack. 'Smash them at sea,' explained Sir Francis. 'We probably won't manage to hit them in harbour - like we did last year - so it must be a sea fight. The last thing we want is thousands of those Popish devils coming ashore with their pikes and artillery and what-not. We wouldn't stand a chance.'

Lord Charles Howard

Howard swatted away a wasp and asked, 'But if we leave English waters with, say, forty ships, Sir Francis, and the Spanish manage to give us the slip, what happens then?'

'Give us the slip?' cried Drake. He swung round to face Lord Charles. 'What crawling Catholic scum has ever managed to give me the slip? Tell me that!'

'Not many, I suppose,' smiled Howard. 'But the idea still worries me.'

Drake's eyes flashed like ships' lanterns in his weather-beaten face. 'Forget your fears, Lord Charles. God is on our side. We are His swordsmen, sent to beat down the Pope's thieving slaves. As

I've told you a thousand times, their ships are no match for ours. Guns are the thing in a sea fight nowadays, and we can out-gun a Spaniard any day.' Howard took a deep breath. 'Very well, Sir Francis. If attack really is the best means of defence, then I suppose we'd better go and find this Armada straight away.'

'God be praised!' exclaimed Drake. 'We'll sail with the morning tide!'

Tom Barnecut had been trying to have a private word with Sir Francis Drake for days. He had even followed him onto Plymouth Hoe and watched him talking with Lord Howard. Now, as the captain came hurrying towards him on his way back to the town, the boy saw his chance. 'Excuse me, sir,' he called boldly, 'but I'm at your service!'

Tom Barnecut

'Eh? What's that, boy?' Drake kept up his steady stride down the grassy slope. 'I'm in a hurry.'

Half-running, Tom fell in beside him. 'Please may I serve with you on the *Revenge*, sir? I want to fight the Spaniard.'

Sir Francis Drake

Drake looked at him out of the corner of his eye. He seemed a strong enough lad.

'Name?' he barked.

'Tom Barnecut, sir. Cornish, sir, of Polperro.'

Drake nodded. 'Age?'

Tom hesitated for half a second. 'Sixteen, sir.' Drake flashed him an angry glance.

'Well, I'll be sixteen next year.'

'That's better. Served at sea?'

'Father's a fisherman, sir.'

'Right. Know the Holy Book? What's the Second Commandment?'

Tom was glad he had paid attention in church. 'We are not to have idols or graven images, like the Papists fill their churches with, sir.'

'Well said, Tom lad! A man after my own heart. I'll see you aboard the *Revenge* before night fall.'

Tom could hardly believe his ears. As Drake strode off into the town, the boy knelt on the

'Please may I serve with you on
the *Revenge*, sir?'

grass and thanked God for his good fortune. He was happier and more excited than he had ever been in his life. Not only was he going to fight the Spaniard, but he was going to do so under the command of his greatest hero - Sir Francis Drake. He'd be the envy of all Polperro!

CHAPTER THREE

'AN AMAZING SIGHT'

The 500-ton *Revenge* was the finest ship Tom had ever been on. Not only was she huge, but she was of the latest design - long, sleek and packed with 70 tons of cannon that fired through portholes set in her sides.

Tom found he had been taken on as a ship's boy, a Jack-of-all trades who spent his time scurrying about with messages, serving food and drink, and doing odd jobs for Drake and the other officers. It was tough work, nowhere near as exciting or glamorous as Tom had thought it would be. But he stuck at it without complaining, and was soon accepted as a regular member of the crew. They called him 'Tom Thumb' or 'Thumby' because he was the smallest person on board.

The *Revenge* and the rest of the English fleet made their way slowly south until it was only sixty miles from the Spanish coast. Drake searched the horizon for a sign of the Armada. He was itching for a fight. But after they had been at sea for two weeks, the wind swung round to the south and the fleet was forced to return to Plymouth.

Drake noticed Tom's disappointment as the familiar English coastline came into sight. 'Cheer up, Thumby!' he said with a smile. 'If it's Spaniards you want to see, then you won't have long to wait now.'

Tom looked confused. 'Why not, sir? Surely we've left them behind us?'

'Think, lad! Think!' the Captain explained. 'Wind's southerly, blowing towards England. Who wants such a breeze, eh?'

'Ah! The Spaniards, sir. Them and their Armada.'

'Aye, Thumby! This wind'll bring them right under our noses in no time. Just you see if it doesn't!'

Tom Barnecut

Sir Francis Drake

Sir Francis was right. On 19 July, 120 Spanish ships were sighted off the Cornish coast. The Armada had arrived! All along the south coast warning beacons were lit, carrying the news to London and the Queen herself. In Plymouth, where most of the fleet lay, sailors hurried aboard their ships and worked furiously to take on stores and ammunition.

Sailors hurried aboard their ships and
worked furiously to take on stores and
ammunition.

That night, because the wind was against them, the English fleet had to be pulled out of harbour using their anchors. It was a back-breaking task. The sailors carried an anchor upwind in a rowing boat, cast it into the water, then hauled the warship up to it before starting all over again. To keep their spirits up, the men sang slow, sentimental sea-songs that brought Tom close to tears.

Old Jack Pugh, who had sailed round the world with Drake, noticed the boy's glistening eyes. 'Save your weeping, young Tom,' he advised. 'There'll be fighting before the week's out. Then, by God, you'll have sorrows enough to cry about.' Tom wiped his eyes on his sleeve and tried not to think about what Old Jack had said.

Old Jack Pugh

The Armada came into view the following afternoon. It was an amazing sight, more majestic and awe-inspiring than anything the Englishmen, even Drake, had seen before. The Spanish vessels, well over 100 of them, were sailing in a gigantic crescent almost three miles wide. There were stately galleons, wallowing transports, galleasses with oars as well as sails, and skipping pinnaces. Flags and pennants fluttered from every mast. 'Strange that the Devil should look so fine,' muttered Drake when he saw the great arc of ships sweeping slowly towards him.

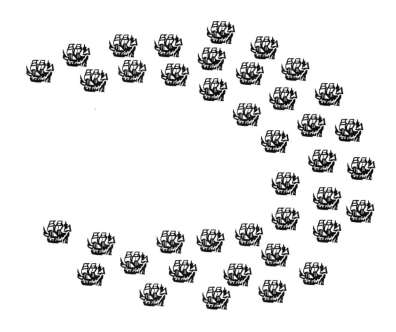

Tom turned to Old Jack and whispered, 'Are we going to attack them now, Jack?'

Jack shook his head. 'Not if I know Captain Drake, boy. You don't close with the enemy till you've the wind at your back. That way you're in control, see?'

'But the wind's from the south-west, behind the Spaniard and in our faces,' Tom replied. 'So what're we going to do? They might attack us.'

Old Jack gave him a toothless grin. 'Do, boy? All you and me have to do is trust in God and Captain Drake. They'll have a plan, don't you worry. Them two always gets it right.'

CHAPTER FOUR

'CREEPING UP IN THE NIGHT'

As night fell, the Duke of Medina-Sidonia, Captain-General of the Ocean Sea, watched until the English coastline became no more than a dark smudge on the horizon, then went down to his cabin for dinner. So far, he thought, so good.

His seasickness, terrible for the first few days, had left him. Although he had been forced to leave some unseaworthy galleys behind, he had brought the rest of his fleet safely into the English Channel. And now he was only a few days' sailing from his meeting with Parma. He sent a servant to find Secretary Carlos.

Alonso, Duke of Medina-Sidonia

Carlos

Carlos was not happy. He was neither a strong man nor a brave one, and the long sea voyage had upset his stomach, ruined his appetite and shattered his nerves. He had lost a lot of weight.

As he stood before his master, the Duke noticed that he had a twitch above his right eyebrow. 'Are you alright, Mr Secretary?' he asked kindly. 'You look particularly anxious this evening.'

'Thank you, Your Grace, but there is nothing wrong with me that will not be cured by a lung-full of pure Spanish air,' Carlos answered. He lifted a hand to his brow to try to stop the twitch. 'I am just a little anxious to think that Drake, the son of the Devil, is out there watching me.'

Duke Alonso smiled. 'He won't harm you, Mr Secretary, I promise. Now would you please take down some letters, then ask Flores to join me for dinner?'

Diego Flores

Diego Flores was the senior officer on the *San Martin*, the Duke's flagship. His job was to advise the Captain-General of the Ocean Sea on matters of seamanship. A battle-hardened veteran, Flores had fought the English before, though without much success. Even so, his judgement was sound, his knowledge of the sea first-class. The Duke was pleased to hear, therefore, that in Flores's opinion the English had been caught out of position. With the wind in the direction it was, the Armada was out of danger for some time.'And even if they try to get at us,' he reckoned, 'our formation will make an all-out attack almost impossible.'

'Excellent!' smiled the Duke, taking a sip of wine. 'So in a few days' time we'll be snug in harbour and loading up the Duke of Parma's soldiers.'

'As long as someone has remembered to tell them we're coming, Your Grace,' Flores added quietly.

The two men spent the rest of the meal chatting happily about what they would do when England was conquered. Flores said he hoped King Philip would make him Duke of Portsmouth.

That night, soothed by the gentle rocking of the *San Martin*, Duke Alonso soon fell asleep. He dreamed he was back at Lucar, walking among the olive groves. But something was wrong. The olives made a great banging noise as they fell from the trees. The banging went on and on, until the Duke realised that he was awake and someone was hammering at the door of his cabin. He lifted himself onto his elbow and asked whoever it was to enter. In burst Carlos, half-dressed and panting like a stranded fish.

'Mr Flores begs your pardon, Your Grace, but he wants you on deck immediately!' he cried.

The Duke raised his hand. 'Calm down, Mr Secretary, and tell me what's going on. I'm sure this wildness is not necessary.'

Carlos

'It's the infidels!' wailed Carlos, wringing his hands like old sheets in the wash.

'They've crept up on us in the night. By magic, I'm sure. I knew they were in league with the Devil. O Mother of God, help us! My old bones will be food for Protestant fish!'

As soon as the Duke had managed to calm Carlos down, he clambered up on deck and looked about him. It was just as his secretary had said. Somehow, during the night, the English had managed to work their way upwind of the Armada.

The Duke turned to Flores. 'How did they manage it?' he asked.

The officer shrugged. 'Good seamanship, I suppose. But at this minute, Your Grace, that is

In burst Carlos, half-dressed and panting
like a stranded fish.

not important. What we need to know is what we are going to do.'

'Why?'

'Because, Your Grace, it is clear that any moment now we're going to find ourselves under attack!'

CHAPTER FIVE

'I SUGGEST WE PRAY'

The battle off Plymouth on 31 July gave the Duke of Medina-Sidonia a taste of what was to come. For four hours the English cruised up and down past the ships on the edge of the Armada. They fired broadside after broadside, but never came close enough for the Spanish to board them.

Alonso, Duke of Medina-Sidonia

Even so, the Duke was quite pleased with the way things turned out. His fleet had stuck to his orders, held its formation and continued on towards its destination. Several ships suffered serious damage, but none was sunk by enemy fire. Two, however, were lost through accidents. The *San Salvador* blew up when one of her crew dropped a match onto a stack of gunpowder barrels. And another powerful vessel, the *Rosario*, was badly damaged in a collision and had to be abandoned.

Carlos had remained hiding below decks throughout the battle. When the gunfire finally died away and he crept back into the fresh air, he found his master in good spirits.

'Ah! At last, Mr Secretary!' he called when he saw him. 'Did you enjoy the fight?'

Carlos stammered something about having had a headache then asked, 'So did we win, Your Grace?'

'Not win,' replied the Duke, 'but we beat them off. Remember what they called the Armada back in Spain? "Invincible!" Not such a bad title, was it, Mr Secretary?'

Carlos

Carlos did not seem convinced. 'Maybe, Your Grace. But what happens now?' he asked nervously.

'More of the same, until we link up with the Duke of Parma.'

Carlos shuddered. 'And may I ask where and when that will be, Your Grace? Has the Duke of Parma contacted us?' Seeing a shadow pass over his master's face, the Secretary knew the answer even as he spoke. There was still no news from the Netherlands. Until it came, the Armada did not know exactly where it was going.

Things went on like this for a week. The Duke took the Armada steadily up the Channel with the English snapping at his heels but doing no real damage. Eventually, on 6 August, the Spanish anchored off the French Channel port of Calais.

Flores was uneasy. 'We are very exposed, Your Grace,' he warned that evening, watching the English fleet anchoring downwind of him. 'The tides run like horses here. There are dangerous shoals and sandbanks, too. Further north, off the Netherlands coast, it's even worse. And that's the direction the wind usually blows in these parts.'

Diego Flores

Alonso, Duke of Medina-Sidonia

The Captain-General of the Ocean Sea shared his anxiety, but he refused to let it show. 'Come on, Flores! Cheer up!' he said briskly. 'Don't lose heart now we've made it this far. The Duke of Parma must know where we are, and any moment he'll let us know the arrangements for taking his army on board. Then I'll put in a word with the King to see you made Duke of Portsmouth. That's a promise.' Flores smiled weakly and went to check the *San Martin's* anchors.

At breakfast time the following morning a boat finally came out from the shore with letters from Parma. The news was grim. The General's forces would not be ready for days, perhaps even a week.

Duke Alonso swore under his breath and called for Carlos. 'This is serious, Mr Secretary. We must get a message back to Parma begging him to get a move on.'

'Do you mean "begging", Your Grace?' Carlos questioned politely.

The Duke looked at him steadily. 'Yes, I mean begging, and pleading, and imploring - anything to get us out of here as quickly as possible.' He turned to Flores. 'Your advice, please, sir. You know the situation: what do we do now?'

'Come on, Flores! Cheer up!'

Flores thought for a moment. 'If we run with the wind up the coast, we could get into all kinds of trouble. If we stay here, the English will attack us. So I suggest we pray. Pray as we have never done before for the wind to change.'

The Duke frowned. 'And if our prayers are not answered?'

'In that case, Your Grace, we must be ready to fight off fire ships.'

CHAPTER SIX

'SINK THE ARMADA!'

Tom Barnecut sat cross-legged on the deck of the *Revenge* and gazed across the water at the anchored Armada. He was trying to work out his feelings.

Tom Barnecut

The last week had been the most exciting of his short life, but it had also been a great shock. War at sea was not what he had imagined. Instead of glory, it was a nightmare of thundering cannon, screams and dreadful cruelty. Having witnessed unspeakable horrors, he had made up his mind to return to Polperro as soon as possible and work with his father as a fisherman. He had seen enough of war to know that it was not for him.

Tom's feelings towards his hero, Drake, had changed, too. True, the great man had shown amazing seamanship and daring. But he had also shown another side of his personality, one that Tom had not known about. Greed.

After the first day's fighting, for example, Sir Francis had disobeyed Lord Howard's orders. Instead of leading the fleet, he had taken the *Revenge* off to capture the disabled *Rosario*. He had plundered valuables and money worth thousands of ducats. The loot should have been handed over to the Queen, but most of it somehow disappeared into the Captain's quarters. The crew were given enough to make sure they kept quiet.

Sir Francis Drake

No, Tom thought, Sir Francis is not a hero. The Spanish, he realised, were not that far from the mark when they called him a pirate. But perhaps in time of war such men were necessary? Tom tried to imagine what it was like for the Spanish sailors, trapped on board their ships far from home. To his surprise, he found himself feeling sorry for them.

Later, when it was dark, Tom was joined on the deck by Old Jack. 'Something's afoot,' he muttered. 'Captain's been dashing about like a ship's cat in a rats' nest.'

Old Jack Pugh   **Tom Barnecut**

'What's he up to, Jack?'

'Well, I reckon he don't want to go at them Spanish close to shore. Too risky. So he's going to drive them out to sea. He'll use fire ships, most likely.'

'Fire ships? What are they?' Tom asked.

Jack clicked his tongue. 'You mean to say you don't know what fire ships is? Well, they's - ' He paused and looked up. While they had been talking, an eerie red glow had appeared in the night sky. 'That's what fire ships is!' he cried, standing up and pointing towards the light.

Eight small ships, stuffed full of tar, spare timber and anything else that burned, had been launched towards the enemy fleet. Some distance off, their crews had set light to them and escaped in rowing boats. Now the wind and tide were carrying the burning vessels straight towards the heart of the anchored Armada. Even from a distance, Tom could see the effect the floating fireballs were having.

Tom Barnecut

A few brave vessels tried unsuccessfully to get hold of the fire ships with hooks and pull them away. Many large galleons simply cut their anchor cables and made for the open sea. There were several collisions. One large warship ran aground. In short, the Spanish fleet was in chaos.

As dawn broke, Drake called his men on deck. Tom stood beside the mainmast and listened to his Captain's words: 'Protestant

'That's what fire ships is!'

Englishmen! Almighty God has delivered the Papists into our hands. This is the hour we have been waiting for. The *Revenge* will lead the attack, and our mission is simple: "Sink the Armada!"'

Even Tom couldn't resist a cheer.

CHAPTER SEVEN

THE BATTLE OF GRAVELINES

'It's going to be a hot fight, Tom lad,' cried Drake. 'Be ready with your bandages and water. By God, they'll be needed!' The Captain spoke without taking his eyes off a large Spanish galleon with which the *Revenge*,

Tom Barnecut

followed by several other English warships, was closing fast.

Tom's job was to help with first aid. It was dangerous work. He had to remain on deck, a target for enemy gunners, ready to run to the help of the wounded. With no training, there wasn't much he could do except wash the wounds and try to stop the bleeding. Squatting down at the foot of the mainmast, he clung tightly onto his bucket of water and roll of linen bandages to stop himself shaking with fear.

When the Spanish vessel was about 400 metres off, Drake suddenly shouted, 'It's her alright, men! The *San Martin*! There's a target for you, gunners: the Papist flagship with the Duke of Medina himself on board! Hold your fire till I give the command, then blast the devil out of the water! A gold crown for the man that kills the Duke!'

The *San Martin* was broadside on to the *Revenge*, waiting. 300 metres ... 200 ... 100.

'Bring her round!' cried Drake. The *Revenge* swung about so she was parallel to the enemy. 'Ready: shoot!'

First the bow cannon, then the whole of the *Revenge*'s starboard broadside poured shot into the *San Martin*. Seconds later, the Spaniard replied. The smoke-filled air shook to the sound of gunfire, splintering wood and cries of pain. Tom saw a man tumble from the rigging onto the deck and ran to help him.

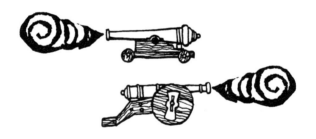

It was Old Jack. A musket ball had passed clean through his chest, and his left arm was twisted beneath him. With a pounding heart, Tom tried to stop the bleeding with a bandage. It was hopeless. Jack opened his eyes for a moment. His lips moved, but no sound came. Then he fell back onto the deck.

Tom saw a man tumble from the rigging
onto the deck.

Tom's throat was as dry as paper. He stooped down to take a drink from his bucket.

At that moment, a cannon ball struck the mast above him, sending a hail of sharp splinters onto the deck. Tom felt a pain in his right leg and glanced down to see a large piece of wood, half as long as his arm, sticking out of his thigh.

He gritted his teeth and dragged himself into a corner below the bridge. There, alone and in great pain, he waited.

Tom lay unnoticed while the battle raged around him. Off the port of Gravelines, just north of Calais, the Spanish received a dreadful pounding. Three of their ships were lost, and many of the others so badly damaged that they were at the mercy of the wind and waves. When, the following day, the wind shifted to the south-west, they fled north.

The English fleet followed, but did not have enough ammunition left to do further damage. A few days later, the battered Spanish vessels were hit by storms and driven up the North Sea towards Scotland. There was now no chance of them returning to join up with the Duke of Parma. The Invincible Armada was beaten.

Tom was taken to the ship's surgeon just after midday. Although his wound looked bad, it was not too serious. After the surgeon had bandaged it up, he handed Tom a small bottle. 'Drink this, Thumby,' he grinned, 'and you won't feel a thing.' Tom looked blank.

'It's a Dutch drink called "burnt wine" or "brandy" - great for killing pain.'

Tom opened the bottle and took a swig. Ugh! He had never tasted anything more revolting, and spat it out.

'So you don't like the sailors' drink?' said a familiar voice behind him. Tom looked up to see the Captain standing over him.

Tom Barnecut   **Sir Francis Drake**

'No, sir,' said Tom. 'Brandy's not for me.'

Drake looked at him for a moment, then said, 'I've been watching you, Tom lad, and I don't think fighting's for you either, is it?'

'No, sir. I'm grateful you gave me chance, but I think I'm more fisher than fighter.'

Drake smiled. 'Honestly spoken. Well, you've done your bit for your country and I'll see you get safely back to Cornwall when you're well enough to travel.'

When the Captain had gone, Tom lay back on the hard boards of the deck and closed his eyes. Well, he thought, maybe Sir Francis is not such a bad fellow after all!

CHAPTER EIGHT

'THE VOYAGE HOME!'

The Captain-General of the Ocean Sea stood looking out over the grey waters of the North Sea. What was he to do? Flores said the Armada could not return to the Netherlands. He had lost seven large warships and hundreds of sailors. The *San Martin* was little more than a

Alonso, Duke of Medina-Sidonia

floating wreck, and the rest of his fleet was not much better. Trusted with a great enterprise, the Duke had let down his king, his country and the Roman Catholic faith. Should he jump into the sea and drown himself? Or take his ship back and go down fighting? That would be the honourable way to go.

He turned to Carlos standing beside him. For the first time in weeks, he noticed, the man was smiling! 'Are you amused by our failure, Mr Secretary?' snapped the Duke. Carlos' smile vanished. 'No, Your Grace! I was only thinking of home,' he cried.

'Home and disgrace?'

'Disgrace? Not at all, sir. You have brought a great fleet across the oceans, beaten off the

53

Protestant pirates, and now you are leading it, most of it, anyway, safely back home. Your Grace, you are a hero.'

'And the invasion of England? Was it heroic to fail in that?'

'Hardly your fault, Your Grace,' Carlos replied quickly. 'You did your part by bringing the Armada to the Channel. You could not have done more.' He shivered and wrapped his cloak around his thin shoulders. 'And, if I may say so, Your Grace, England was not worth having anyway. A cold, wet land, full of infidels and barbarians. His Majesty is better off without it.'

Put like that, the Duke thought, things did not sound so bad. He decided not to drown himself, or go down fighting. Instead, he'd try to get as many ships as possible safely back to Spain.

Carlos

Now he knew what he had to do, the Duke's energy returned. He hanged one of the captains who had disobeyed his battle orders and put the others under arrest. To save food and water, he ordered all horses and mules to be thrown overboard. Every crew member, even the Duke

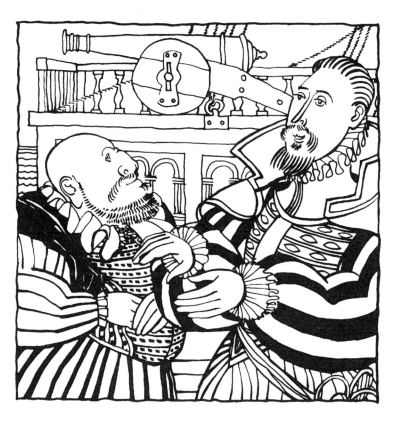

'And the invasion of England?
Was it heroic to fail in that?'

himself, had to survive on a daily ration of biscuit, water and wine.

Although the Duke tried hard to hold the Armada together for the long journey home round Scotland and Ireland, the weather was against him. August that year was unusually wet and stormy. Worse still, the wind came mainly from the south-west, making progress toward Spain extremely difficult.

By the end of the month the Armada had scattered, leaving most captains struggling on their own to get their ships home.

After the *San Martin* had finally rounded Ireland and was sailing south-east for Spain, the Duke relaxed a little. He asked Secretary Carlos and Diego Flores to his cabin.

'I wish to thank you for your help during this terrible voyage,' he said. 'And when we get home, which I'm sure we will now, I'll see that all Spain hears of your service.'

Flores thanked him warmly, but Carlos' face creased with horror. 'Oh no, Your Grace!' he cried. 'Please don't mention me to anyone!'

The Duke was amazed. 'I beg your pardon, Your Grace,' Carlos explained, 'but if you praise me, I might be asked to go to sea again! And I think I'd rather die!'

The Duke sighed. 'So would I, Mr Secretary. But don't worry. After what has happened, I don't think either of us will be asked to set foot on board a ship ever again!'

WHAT HAPPENED NEXT?

A SPANISH DISASTER

The Duke of Medina-Sidonia had about 130 ships when he sailed for England. Only 60 made it safely back home, and many of these were too badly damaged to be repaired. The human casualties were even more shocking. Of the 27,000 sailors and soldiers who went with the Armada, almost half (15,000) died in the fighting or from disease and shipwreck. Compared with these, the English losses were tiny. The Queen and her people hailed the defeat of the Armada as a great triumph, and England celebrated its anniversary for many years.

MORE ARMADAS, MORE FAILURES

In 1589, the year after the Armada, the English fleet launched an attack on Spain and Portugal. It achieved nothing. Sir Francis Drake had other failures, too, and died of disease in the Caribbean in 1596. Meanwhile, King Philip pressed ahead with his plan to invade England. In 1596 and 1597 he prepared two more Armadas. They were even more unlucky than the first - they were driven back by storms even before they reached the Channel.

PEACE AT LAST

When King Philip died in 1598, Spain was still the most powerful country in Europe. But it had not managed to conquer England or overcome the Dutch, and its period of greatness was rapidly coming to a close. Elizabeth I died five years later (1603). Her successor, James VI and I, was a man of peace and soon brought the war with Spain to an end. After the death of the Duke of Parma in 1592, the Spanish had found it difficult to make any headway against the Dutch. When the Spanish and Dutch signed a truce in 1609, more than twenty years after the defeat of the Armada, the fighting finally stopped.

HOW DO WE KNOW?

ARCHIVES
Historians put together the story of the Spanish Armada by searching through archives in Spain and England. Archives are collections of papers - things like letters, reports, bills, orders and so on - remaining from that time. These papers do not always agree with one another. Most people do not admit that they made mistakes or behaved badly. Drake, for example, did not say he disobeyed orders when he went to seize the damaged *Rosario*! We have to see what others wrote to find out the truth. Luckily, Philip II was a very efficient man who kept careful records of everything. This makes the Spanish archives more useful than the English ones.

OTHER EVIDENCE
We can also learn about the Spanish Armada from objects. Portraits show us what people looked like. Pictures of things like cannon and ships are also useful. Obviously, the ships themselves largely disappeared centuries ago. But divers have found the wrecks of Spanish galleons around the

coast of Britain and Ireland. The wood has mostly rotted away, but metal objects remain. Interestingly, some galleons sank with plenty of cannon balls on board. Perhaps this shows that they fled without putting up much of a fight? Or had they run out of gunpowder? Questions like this may never be answered.

BOOKS

The easiest way for you to find out more about the Spanish Armada is to look in one of the many history books written for children about this period of history. You probably have several in your school library, and there will be more in the local town library. Some of these are general books about Tudor England. Others are biographies (life stories) of famous people, such as Elizabeth I and Sir Francis Drake. You may find a book just about the Spanish Armada. The two (adult) books which contain the most up-to-date information are *The Spanish Armada* by C Martin and G Parker, (London, 1988) and *Francis Drake* by John Cummins, (London, 1995).

NEW WORDS

Armada Large fleet of warships
Beacon Signal fire
Broadside All the guns down one side of a ship
Crown English coin worth 5 shillings or one quarter of a pound
Ducat Valuable gold or silver coin
Galleass Ship powered by oars and sails
Galleon Large 16th-century sailing ship
Galley Large ship powered by rows of oars
Graven image Old-fashioned phrase for a carved picture or statue
Hoe Piece of land jutting into the sea
Infidel Slang word for someone of a different religious faith
New World North and South America
Pennant Small flag
Pike Long spiked weapon like a spear but not for throwing
Pinnace Type of small, ocean-going sailing vessel
Porthole Watertight window in the side of a ship
Popish Slang expression for Roman Catholic
Ration Allowance of food
Spoils Valuables stolen by victorious soldiers
Tavern Pub

TIME LINE

1555   Philip II becomes King of Spain
1558   Elizabeth I becomes Queen of England
1567   Dutch rebellion against Spanish rule begins
1568   Mary Queen of Scots a prisoner of
          Elizabeth I
1577-81 Francis Drake sails round the world,
          attacking Spanish ships and possessions
1585   England and Spain unofficially at war
          Philip II plans to invade England
1587   Mary Queen of Scots executed
          Drake raids Spanish port of Cadiz
1588   **February** Duke of Medina-Sidonia
          takes command of the Armada
          May Armada sails from Lisbon, Portugal
          (then in Spanish hands)
          July Armada reaches English Channel and
          fights its way to Calais
          July 29 Armada badly damaged at Battle
          of Gravelines
          August Medina-Sidonia decides to return
          home round the north of Scotland
          Autumn Surviving Armada ships return home
1589   Unsuccessful English attack on Spain and
          Portugal
1593   Duke of Parma dies
1596   Second Armada fails, Sir Francis Drake dies
1597   Third Armada fails
1598   Philip II dies
1603   Elizabeth I dies
1604   England and Spain make peace
1609   Spanish and Dutch sign a truce